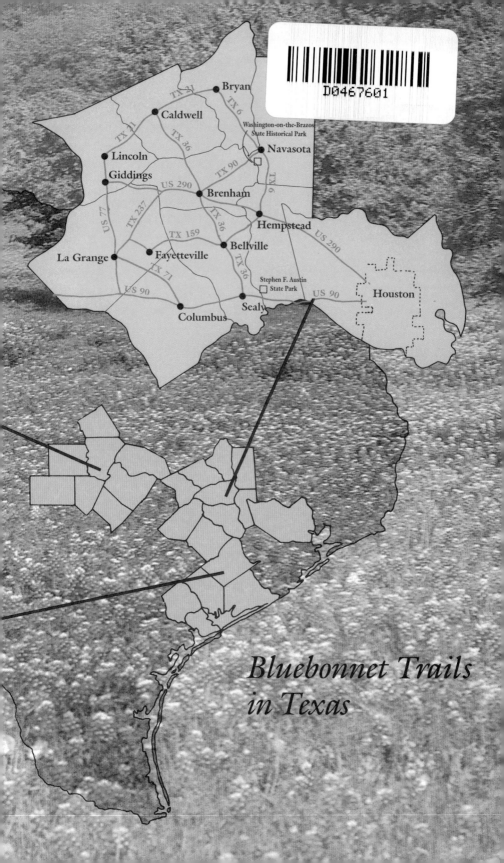

D0467601

Bryan

TX 21

Caldwell

TX 6

Washington-on-the-Brazos
State Historical Park

TX 36

Navasota

Lincoln

TX 21

Giddings

US 290

Brenham

TX 90

TX 6

US 77

TX 237

TX 36

Hempstead

US 290

TX 159

Bellville

La Grange

Fayetteville

TX 36

Stephen F. Austin
State Park

TX 71

US 90

Sealy

US 90

Houston

Columbus

Bluebonnet Trails
in Texas

The Texas Bluebonnet

The Texas Bluebonnet

BY JEAN ANDREWS

UNIVERSITY OF TEXAS PRESS, AUSTIN

To my father, HERBERT ANDREWS,
who at age 20 became a naturalized Texan. During the
following sixty years he never learned to like cornbread but he
loved "his" bluebonnets . . . so much so that he allowed them
to fill his pastures, knowing that his cattle wouldn't eat them.

From . . . a daughter who is fifth-generation Texan on the
distaff side with real bluebonnet blood in her veins.

He made me proud to be "half-Yankee."

International Standard Book Number 0-292-70758-4
Library of Congress Catalog Card Number 86-6982
Copyright © 1986 by Dr. Jean Andrews Smith

All rights reserved
Printed in Japan

Second Printing, 1987

Requests for permission to reproduce material
from this work should be sent to
Permissions, University of Texas Press,
Box 7819, Austin, TX 78713-7819.

Except where specific credit is given, all photographs in
this book are by the author.

Contents

Introduction

*B*luebonnet time isn't just springtime, it's a time "when the sky falls on Texas," as A. L. Morgan wrote. It is also a time of celebration—a celebration not of a victory or a foe vanquished, not of love, or wealth, or a deed of great valor, but a celebration of transcendent nature. It is a time in Texas when the land and the sky, the lakes and the rivers, and the ocean are blue. It all runs together and envelops us in its majesty and mystique. A celebration of being alive to glimpse again that azure panorama and be enveloped by it, each in our own way, as a child who can't resist the primordial urge to roll in the luxuriant blue robe that is cloaking his universe. Is it any wonder that no artist has been able to capture the essence of that celebration? It is beyond the capacity of humans to portray on canvas or with film what we have seen or felt in those few weeks in the heart of Texas when heaven and earth become one with mortals. Suzanne Winkler expressed it aptly: "Things of great beauty that also bear the burden of being common are difficult, if not impossible, to praise." I can add "or paint" without fear of contradiction.

Perhaps it is good that the spectacle lasts but a few weeks so that we do not become accustomed to it and we still have the vision to dream of and look forward to next year, and the next.

I can only agree with J. Frank Dobie, when he confessed that "no other flower—for me at least—brings such upsurging of the spirit and at the same time such restfulness." It is "a passion of blossom, a splendor of spread," according to Mary Daggett Lake. Margaret Bell Houston asked, in "Song from the Traffic," "Is any blue so blue?" And so far we have not even whispered of its fragrance, which subtly permeates the warm spring air.

When did Texans first begin noticing, and then revering, this anything but humble endemic wild flower? The first to observe the bluebonnet were trained European naturalists sent to this new land of Texas to collect yet unknown specimens of the plant and animal kingdoms.

3492

Pub by S.Curtis. Glazenwood Essex May 1. 1836.

Swan Sc.

In 1826 a twenty-year-old Franco-Swiss botanical explorer, Jean Louis Berlandier, was shipped to Mexico by his professor, the famous naturalist Augustin Pyrame de Candolle, as the botanist for the Mexican boundary commission that was attempting to establish the borders between the Republic of Mexico and the United States of America.

What may be the first recorded observation of the Texas bluebonnet can be found in the copious notes made by Berlandier in his journal of the expedition into Mexico (which included Texas at that time). On April 13, 1828, he departed from Ciudad de Bexar (San Antonio) on a journey to Nacogdoches. The first night the company bedded down at the Arroyo del Salado, about five miles from the presidio of the Alamo. That evening he wrote: "The fields, strewn with flowers, were yet only a small thing compared with what we saw in the upper regions of Texas. A lupine, verbena, delphinium, some lilies, and a great many evening primroses contrasted with the tender green of the grasses, from which sprang flowers of various colors."

Five or six years after Berlandier's trip, Thomas Drummond, a Scottish naturalist, ventured to Texas under the sponsorship of Sir William Jackson Hooker, who was later keeper of the Royal Botanic Gardens at Kew, England. Hooker used material collected under hazardous conditions in that raw new land by Berlandier and Drummond to describe and name the two new lupines they had discovered.

Ten years after Hooker's description of the Texas lupine had been published, the methodical German geologist Ferdinand von Roemer made notes on the lupines he saw near Gonzales while on an eighteen-month collecting expedition to Texas, saying, "They covered the hills with color." As yet they were not called bluebonnets.

Other than the reports of these three trained naturalists, a search of the literature for further evidence failed to produce a clue. Even the highly observant Frederick Law Olmsted, who

Illustration that accompanied Hooker's description of *Lupinus*. See page 64 for the solution of a 150-year-old bluebonnet mystery. Photograph from the Harry Ransom Humanities Research Center, University of Texas at Austin.

seemed to miss nothing as he rode his trusted horse through the limitless expanses of Texas, failed to make note of the bluebonnet. He mentions the grapevine and Spanish moss, even spending some space on the "mesquit," describing it as "a short thin tree of the locust tribe, whose branches are thick set with thorns, and bears, except in this respect, a close resemblance to a straggling, neglected peach-tree." So we know he looked closely, but not a word of recognition to something as conspicuous as a prairie covered with bluebonnets. In Marilyn McAdams Sibley's reviews of the accounts of journeys of many early travelers, we are told that "history passed in review along the highways of Texas in the century 1761–1860," but evidently no one seemed to notice, or if they did they failed to leave records of their impression of our little blue friend.

Could it be that the bluebonnet was not so widespread or so plentiful during the first 150 years of Texas history? I don't think so. Those first hardy newcomers to the vast region we now know as Texas were just too busy with other things. The elements, in the form of blue northers and hurricanes, occupied their attention, along with hostile, mounted Indians, to name but two diverting factors.

After those intrepid pioneer Texians constructed shelter from the weather, they assured themselves of their next meal of corn pone and fried fatback with an occasional bit of game, a few vegetables, or an egg or two. Then they went on to "solve" their Indian problems. They were now ready to look at the big new territory. Or were they? Not just yet. Not before they had wrested Texas from Mexico as the sounds of the Alamo, Goliad, and San Jacinto rang in their ears; shaped it into a recognized republic; been admitted to the United States of America as the Lone Star State; settled their border dispute with their neighboring republic in the Mexican War of 1846; fought and bled with the Confederate States of America for what they believed to be their state's rights; endured the humiliation of Reconstruction; established far-spreading ranching empires; and discovered an ocean of black gold—oil, were they ready for some of the niceties of life . . . such as, flowers. Namely, a state flower.

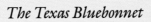

The Texas Bluebonnet

Adopting a State Flower

Back in 1901, March blew in across the plains of Texas in its usual blustery fashion to be met with an equal quantity of blustering hot air in the chambers of the state legislature. As in spring throughout time thoughts have turned to flowers, so had the musings of our elected leaders. Choosing the state flower was on the agenda. The previous year the Senate had passed a resolution with little conflict. But, in the House, debates were flying fast and furious as one legislator launched his appeal for his favorite, to be followed by more eloquent protestations of the virtues of yet another. Phil Clement of Mills pleaded the case of the open cotton boll, which he likened to "the white rose of commerce." John Nance Garner, later the vice-president of the United States, jousted in behalf of the prickly-pear cactus flower. Although the youthful politico was not successful in gaining the title for his chosen bloom, he went to his grave with the sobriquet he so gallantly earned that day, "Cactus Jack" Garner.

Then up to the podium strode John M. Green of Cuero. As Green made his appeal for the beautiful bluebonnet, calls came from the floor asking, "What the devil is a bluebonnet?" Someone replied that it was that blue flower that looked like those old-timey sunbonnets the pioneer Texas women wore in futile attempts to protect themselves from the burning sun and winds of Texas. Another replied, "You must mean '*el conejo*'." "The rabbit" was a name used by the Mexicans because the waving white tip reminded them of the bobbing tail of a cottontail rabbit. "No, no, no," roared another. "He's referring to what some have called 'buffalo clover'." Yet another rose up to protest that it was the wolf flower, so named by Old World botanists. No one seemed to know just what flower Green had proposed to them or what to call it.

At that point a group of stalwart Texas women rose to the cause and proved Rodgers and Hammerstein's claim that "there is nothing like a dame." The National Society of the Colonial Dames of America in the State of Texas (not to be confused

SANDY WILSON PHOTO

This painting by Mode Walker was the deciding factor in the choice of the bluebonnet state flower of Texas. Measuring 15¾" × 19¾", it hangs in the Colonial Dames of America in the State of Texas Museum at the Neill-Cochran House, 2310 San Gabriel, Austin, Texas.

with other groups of colonial descendants) had originated the idea of using the bluebonnet as the state flower and they were not going to let their favored blossom be left by the roadside for a cactus bloom or cotton boll just because a bunch of representatives didn't know what it was. After a quickly held council of war to devise their tactics, they determined to make a visual appeal to the legislature. A bluebonnet painting was sent for, and one painted by Miss Mode Walker of Austin was carried into the chamber. We are told by Mary Daggett Lake that "deep silence reigned for an instant. Then deafening applause fairly shook the old walls." The bluebonnet had won hands down. It was approved by Governor Joseph D. Sayers on March 7, 1901.

The following is the text of the resolution that made the bluebonnet the state flower of Texas on March 5, 1901.

CONCURRENT RESOLUTION

WHEREAS, *the State of Texas at present has no State flower, and*

WHEREAS, *the National Society of Colonial Dames of America resident in Texas have requested of the Legislature that it adopt the* Lupinus subcarnosus *(generally known as buffalo clover or blue bonnet) as the State flower, therefore,*

BE IT RESOLVED *by the Senate of the State of Texas, the House of Representatives concurring, that* Lupinus subcarnosus *(generally known as buffalo clover or blue bonnet) be and the same is hereby declared to be the State flower of Texas.*

APPROVED *March 7, 1901.*

(NOTE: The enrolled bill shows that the foregoing resolution passed the Senate, no vote given; and passed the House of Representatives, no vote given.)

We shall soon see the reasons for a problem that arose over the designation of *L. subcarnosus* as the state flower. Not only were the legislators confused about the common names by which the bluebonnet was known in 1901, but they also failed to realize that there existed within the borders of Texas several species of bluebonnets and that the one they had specified was not the most common. Seventy years later this confusion was resolved with a resolution.

Lupinus subcarnosus is the delicate low plant that paints the sandy, rolling hills of Texas with waves of azure blue in the early spring. However, some citizens believed it was the least attractive of the Texas bluebonnets. It is highly probable that the ardent legislators did not know that there were six species of bluebonnets in the state, each adding its color to the spring parade. Naturally, given that number, a complication arose. Of the six the consensus of bluebonnet lovers put forward *L. texensis,* the larger, bolder, deeper blue beauty that blankets most of Central Texas and brings painters out all week, not just on Sunday, during bluebonnet season.

For seventy years the argument kicked up dust in the halls of the state Capitol until the politically astute representatives of the wide bluebonnet constituency decided to correct their oversight. In 1971, in order to make certain that they would not be caught in another botanical trap, they covered all their bases in H.C.R. No. 44 without offending the *L. subcarnosus* boosters by offering an additional resolution that would include not only *L. texensis* but also "any other variety of Bluebonnet not heretofore recorded." On March 8, 1971, H.C.R. 44 was signed by Governor Preston Smith. We therefore have six state flowers, with the possibility of others if any new species are discovered or introduced.

Although the bluebonnet has been designated by the Texas Legislature as the official state flower, the plant is not granted any more protection from picking under state law than any other wild flower. A spokesman for the Texas Department of Highways and Public Transportation said state law declares it a misdemeanor to "recklessly damage or destroy" wild flowers along state-owned road rights-of-way. The department discourages the public from disturbing the flowers; however, law enforcement officials normally do not construe casual enjoyment of the plants, including picking, to be "reckless damage and destruction."

It *is* unlawful to pick, dig up, or otherwise damage any plant found in a state or national park. It is recommended that Texans and visitors enjoy the wild flowers without damaging or removing them, in order to allow more people this privilege.

As historian Jack Maguire so aptly wrote, "It's not only the state flower but also a kind of floral trademark almost as well known to outsiders as cowboy boots and the Stetson hat." He goes on to affirm that the "bluebonnet is to Texas what the shamrock is to Ireland, the cherry blossom to Japan, the lily to France, the rose to England and the tulip to Holland."

What a Bluebonnet Is

The bluebonnet is but one of the five thousand or more different species of wild flowers that splash their vivid hues across the vastness we know as Texas in their respective seasons throughout the year. As the ballad of our singing governor, the late W. Lee O'Daniel, goes, you may be on the "plains or the mountains or down where the sea breezes blow," but bluebonnets are one of the prime factors that make the state "the most beautiful land that we know." At the turn of the century when the legislature declared bluebonnets to be the state flower, there was no recorded opposition to *Lupinus subcarnosus*.

The genus *Lupinus* (Lu-pie-nus) is represented in Texas by several species of this winter annual. Of the six presently recognized, *L. subcarnosus* Hooker and *L. texensis* Hooker are more widespread. The first is the original state flower of Texas; however, the latter is sometimes erroneously considered a synonym for the same plant. *Lupinus subcarnosus* is endemic (that is, native to a specific area) to Texas, but *L. texensis* wanders into Coahuila, Mexico; nevertheless, both are our famous Texas bluebonnets and neither occurs naturally any place else in the world, according to M. C. Johnston.

A recognized Lupine authority, B. L. Turner of the University of Texas at Austin, informs us that bluebonnets are probably the most important native rangeland legumes in Central Texas, often occupying hundreds of acres of rolling hillsides during the early spring months. The roots of these legumes are highly nodulated, making them important sources of nitrogen for the soil. *Lupinus texensis* has become a popular ornamental in landscape gardening in many places in the world and most of the material offered by seed suppliers belongs to this species. Both of these species have the same chromosome number and are apparently very closely related taxonomically; however, they are largely confined to different habitats and in the field they are reproductively isolated. Thus they fulfill the criterion of biological species, which are groups of actually or potentially interbreeding natural populations, reproductively isolated from other such groups by geographical, physiological, or ecological barriers.

Lupinus texensis naturally prefers calcareous or clay soils of the Central Texas prairies or the rocky soils of the Edwards Plateau, while *L. subcarnosus* occurs naturally only on the sandy soils of Central Texas, B. A. Schaal writes. Turner states that they do not hybridize in nature, even in habitats that permit their side-by-side occurrence.

Bluebonnets are not self-fertilizing. L. Erbe reported that seed pods are not produced by the florets of *L. texensis* unless the florets have been "worked" by bees or humans. Attracted by the white banner spots on the blue flower, the bumblebee *(Bombus pennsylvanicus)* and the nonnative honeybee *(Apis mellifera)* forage for pollen, which they then deposit on a neighboring plant. Schaal reports that the gene-filled pollen is carried only a short distance from its point of origin; therefore, two plants close together are likely to be more genetically similar than two plants farther apart. This movement of genetic material within a plant population is called the "gene flow."

A natural bluebonnet population consists of about ten thousand plants covering several hectares (3–6 acres) divided into many neighborhoods of forty-two to ninety-five plants.* Random mating occurs within each neighborhood. In the case of *L. texensis* the neighborhood size and gene flow are very restricted, which results in a genetically mixed, or heterogeneous, population.

The five petals of the bluebonnet flower perform separate functions in the reproductive process. The upper petal, or banner, has a white spot to signal a passing bee that dinner is ready and a red spot when dinner is finished. The two side petals protect the lower petals, which are the landing platform for the

---

*Neighborhood size is determined by pollinator (bee) foraging distance and seed dispersal distance.

Mean flight distance: 0.97 ± 0.08 m   Mean seed dispersal: 0.58 ± 0.04 m

A comprehensive discussion of the divergencies in the population biology of these two bluebonnet species can be found in an article by Barbara Schaal, Washington University, St. Louis. In fact, she has done more detailed study of *L. texensis* than any other lupine scholar.

pollinators. These two lower petals meet, forming a keel-like structure, thus protecting the enclosed reproductive organs. When a bee alights on this keel, pollination is triggered and the petals open. This action throws the pollen-bearing reproductive organs against the bee. The bee transports the gene-filled pollen to a nearby flower, thereby establishing a gene flow between the two plants.

You have probably noticed that the banner petals of the blue flowers make a dramatic color change from white to magenta red, and, quite likely, you were told that this was a sign the flower had been pollinated. Not so! That is a common misconception. Actually, bees limit their foraging activity to white-marked flowers and this color change is the bluebonnet's signal that its pollen is no longer fertile. The pollen of the freshly opened bluebonnet flowers germinates readily but its viability decreases daily. By the sixth day little or no germination occurs.

Studies by Schaal and Leverich have shown that the banner spot is going to change from white to magenta whether the flower is visited by a bee or not. Age alone is the determining factor. On the fifth day after the flower opens that spot is going to turn red regardless of what has happened. When this occurs there is less color contrast. The bee is quick to notice nature's signal and doesn't waste its time and energy buzzing around flowers that have had their pollen depleted by earlier kinsmen. Perhaps as another attention getter, the pollen starts out orange, then turns to yellow-white as it ages; consequently, it may not be so "gold" for the bees. Flowers that are not pollinated before the change in banner and pollen color do not set seed.

Among all species of Texas bluebonnets occasional plants with white blossoms appear. These are only albinos (lack normal coloration) of the existing species, not something new. Albino mutants are not pollinated as frequently by insects as are the colored blooms, but those that are produce both white and blue offspring. Consequently, open pollination (in nature) produces few white flowers. To make certain that the seed from an albino bluebonnet will produce white flowers, the flowers would have to be either self-pollinated or crossed by hand with pollen from another white flower. Since we already know that bluebonnets are not self-pollinating, the chances of establishing colonies of white bluebonnets in the wild are few and far between. Not only are there white bluebonnets but a pink bluebonnet also occurs. Look for it in the vicinity of Inks Lake.

The Texas bluebonnet belongs to the legume, or bean, family (Leguminosae/Fabaceae). This is a very large family having many members with high protein levels and nitrogen fixation in roots nodulated with the bacterium *Rhizobium.* Because lupines are able to invade soils low in nitrogen they have become established in disturbed areas. This is the reason why certain species are used as cover crops for the enrichment of agricultural soils. Many species from both the Old World and the New World are employed in horticulture because they have at-

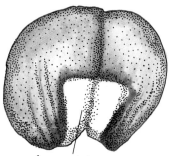

banner spot

banner petal

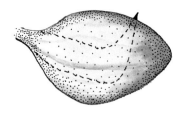

wing petal (2)

tractive flowers of various colors. D. B. Dunn and J. M. Gillett report that a number of lupine species have proved to be poisonous to cattle and sheep, but because of confusion in species names it is difficult to know for certain which ones are highly toxic.

Let's take a closer look at this symbiotic relationship (a partnership of dissimilar organisms) between the soil bacterium *Rhizobium* and the plant genus *Lupinus*. The nitrogen produced through this symbiosis is available to herbivores when eaten and is released and made available to other plants when the bluebonnet decomposes.

Botanists have recently determined that one of the major problems facing legume breeders, agronomists, and plant in-

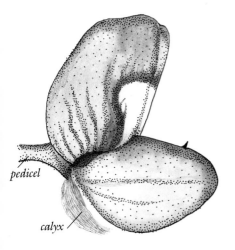

staminal column

keel petal (2)

Parts of a bluebonnet flower, *Lupinus texensis*

troductionists is the influence of the indigenous population of *Rhizobium* on plant performance. Bacteria populations differ among regions and soil types, and any lupine breeding or introduction program in a certain area will involve selection for the most successful symbiotic associations in that location. A. H. Gibson was not surprised to find that many host selections fail to perform in a different region or soil type as well as they do in their original environment. These studies hold considerable implications for those who want to grow bluebonnets. The *Rhizobium* species required for nitrogen fixation in any of the Texas bluebonnets have not been determined at this time. There could be just one or as many as six, depending on whether or not it is species-specific. However, it may be proved that the *Rhizobium* is not so particular as to bluebonnet species but that, instead, it requires a distinct soil type, or both, according to David Northington.

A successful bluebonnet breeding program depends on cultural practices that encourage prompt nodulation so as to reduce the effects of environmental stress on nodule formation and function, states R. J. Roughley. Nodulation is the problem, not germination.

Nitrogen-fixing nodules on the roots of bluebonnets and other legumes are the result of the symbiotic relationship, previously mentioned, between *Rhizobium* and the host plant. H. D. L. Corby explains that the nodule shapes tend to be constant for species, round initially and developing their characteristic shapes later. Flourishing nodules impose such a heavy drain on the parent plant that it is common to find the root much diminished beyond the point of attachment of the nodule.

The lupine nodule differs from those of all other legumes. The rufflike lupinoid nodule is characteristic of the genus *Lupinus,* where it occurs in two forms: one is single and irregularly rounded; the other occurs in clusters.

As a guide to the identification of the six *Lupinus* species found in Texas, the following key and descriptions have been specially prepared for this book by B. L. Turner, author of *The Legumes of Texas.*

Genus: *Lupinus* Linné, 1753
Lupine (Bluebonnet)

Biennials or winter annuals or perennial herbs; forming rosettes in the fall, flowering the next spring; taproots slender. Leaves palmately compound with 1 or 2 to many leaflets; stipules adnate (adherent) to the base of the petiole. Flowers showy, mostly white, blue, or purplish (rarely, yellow), in rather large terminal racemes or spikes; stamens monodelphous (fused into a single unit or tube), anthers of two kinds. Fruit a dry, oblong or linear, somewhat flattened legume with several to numerous, hard seeds. Mature pods split open to release seeds. Base chromosome number $x + 12$ ($2^n = 36, 48$)

A large, complex genus with perhaps 200 species in the temperate regions of North America, South America, and the Mediterranean area of Europe and western Asia.

KEY TO *LUPINUS* SPECIES

1. Plants about 1 foot or less tall; pods 1 inch or less long, 2–4 seeded; El Paso and Jeff Davis counties . . . . *L. concinnus*
1. Plants 1–4 feet tall; pods 2–3 inches long, 5–10 seeded
   2. Flowering scapes usually exceeding the foliage; Big Bend region of Trans-Pecos Texas . . . . *L. havardii*
   2. Flowering scapes not exceeding the foliage
      3. Uncommon perennials of the northern Panhandle or southeastern-most Texas; leaves with 7–19 leaflets
         4. Flowers light to dark blue; plants of southeastern-most Texas . . . . *L. perennis*
         4. Flowers bluish-purple to bicolored; plants of the northern Panhandle of Texas . . . . *L. plattensis*
      3. Abundant winter annuals or biennials of Central Texas: leaves with 5 leaflets
         5. Apex of flowering stalk without a distinct white top; leaflets rounded at apex; wing petals inflated . . . . *L. subcarnosus*
         5. Apex of flowering stalk with a distinct white top; leaflets not rounded at apex; wing petals not inflated. . . . . *L. texensis*

1. DESERT OR ANNUAL LUPINE

Lupinus concinnus Agardh, 1835. *Syn. Gen. Lupin.*, 6

Small erect winter annuals 6−12 inches tall, the stems much-branched below, the lateral branches often recumbent (reclining). Leaves with tawny spreading hairs, the petioles much exceeding the 5−7 leaflets in length. Flowers lavender blue, keel red-tipped, arranged in very short compact spikes but scarcely surpassing the foliage. Pods about 1 inch or less long, about ¼ inch wide, densely pubescent (hairy) with spreading hairs, 2−4 seeded.

A somewhat widespread species occurring in sandy clay or gravelly soils in Trans-Pecos Texas and westward. In Texas it occurs primarily about El Paso and as isolated populations in the Davis Mountains, just east of Fort Davis along Limpia Creek. Flowering primarily in April.

2. CHISOS OR BIG BEND BLUEBONNET

Lupinus havardii S. Watson, 1882. *Proc. Am. Acad. Arts*, XVII, 17: 369

Erect winter annual or biennial mostly 2−3 feet tall, the elongate flowering stalks usually surpassing the foliage. Leaves appressed (pressed closely against), pubescent (with hairs not spreading), the petioles much exceeding the usually 7 leaflets. Flowers blue, loosely arranged along slender flowering stalks. Wing petals not inflated. Pods 2−3 inches long, about ¼ inch wide, densely pubescent with tawny appressed hairs, 8−10 seeded.

Occurring in sandy, silty-clay, or gravelly soils in the Chihuahuan desert regions of Trans-Pecos Texas and adjacent Mexico from 3,500 to 4,500 feet. Flowering primarily in April and May. First collected by Dr. V. Havard in May 1881 near Presidio, Texas, while surveying the Texas-Mexico boundary.

3. PERENNIAL BLUEBONNET

Lupinus perennis Linné, 1753. *Sp. Pl.*, 721

Erect slender perennial to 4 feet tall, the stems arising from wiry underground stems or rhizomes forming small colonies, the flowering stalks about equalling or somewhat shorter than the foliage. Leaves sparsely to moderately pubescent with long spreading hairs, the petioles much longer (2–3 times) than the usually 8–10 leaflets. Flowers light to dark blue, rather tightly formed along the raceme forming an evenly acute apex much in the manner of *L. subcarnosus*. Pods 2–3 inches long, about ⅜ inch wide, much as in *L. plattensis*.

Occurring in southeastern-most Texas extending into the state from a wider distribution in the southeastern United States. It is rare in Texas and has never been reported to occur in large populations as does *L. texensis* or *L. subcarnosus*. Flowering in April and May. First collected in Orange County, Texas, in 1931. Those *L. perennis* occurring in Texas are the variety *austrinus* Shinners 1953.

4. PLAINS BLUEBONNET

Lupinus plattensis S. Watson, 1882. *Proc. Am. Acad. Arts,* XVII: 363

Rather robust perennial to 3 feet tall, the stems arising from slender underground stems or rhizomes, the flowering stalks surpassing the leaves but not excessively so, about ¼–⅓ as long as the foliage. Leaves minutely pubescent with appressed hairs, the petioles exceeding the usually 7 leaflets. Flowers bluish-purple to bicolored, numerous but appearing somewhat whorled along the stout racemes. Pods 2–3 inches long, about ⅜ inch wide, 6–8 seeded.

Known in Texas only from a few populations in deep sandy soils of the Panhandle of Texas, where it perhaps is largely maintained by vegetative reproduction. It is much more widespread and common northward to Canada. Flowering in May and June. First collected in Texas in 1961 by the late D. S. Correll, botanist and author of *The Flora of Texas*.

5. TEXAS BLUEBONNET I

Lupinus subcarnosus Hooker, 1836. *Bot. Mag.,* 63: t. 3467

Very similar to *L. texensis* but lacks the pronounced white tuft of flowers, or cap, at the apex of the raceme that is typical of *L. texensis*. This is readily evident from a distance, even from a fast-moving automobile. The very obtuse or rounded leaflets of *L. subcarnosus* contrast with the apically acute or merely obtuse leaflets of *L. texensis*. Other characters, such as the inflated wing petals (mumps-like) versus the noninflated wing petals in *L. texensis,* further distinguish the two.

Of the two Texas bluebonnets of Central Texas, *L. subcarnosus* is less common and less colorful. Occurring almost always in deep sandy soils, the plants are usually more widely spaced and have fewer basal branches than *L. texensis.* Both of the Texas bluebonnets flower at the same time, March and April; rarely May with rains. First collected in Texas at San Felipe by the early naturalist Drummond in 1835.

6. TEXAS BLUEBONNET II

Lupinus texensis Hooker, 1836. *Bot. Mag.,* 63: t. 3492

Winter annual or biennial 1–2 feet tall, the lower stems usually branching from the base of the primary stem lending a relatively prolonged flowering effect. Leaves pubescent with mostly appressed, soft hairs, the petioles 2–3 times as long as the 5 somewhat acute to obtuse leaflets. Flowers deep blue, with each possessing a pronounced white "eye," which changes to a magenta red; arranged in relatively compact short spikes ¼–⅓ as long as the foliage. Pods 2–3 inches long, about ¼ inch wide, densely pubescent with tawny hairs, seeds usually 6–8 per pod.

Largely endemic to Central Texas, where it occurs on clayey or calcareous soils, often extending into sandy lands occupied by *L. subcarnosus* by "clinging" to the roadsides where packed clay or shell is used to stabilize the roadway. It has been widely dispersed along roadsides throughout Texas by the state's highway department, thereby greatly extending its natural range. Flowering in March and April; rarely May with rains. First collected in Texas at Bejar (now San Antonio) by Berlandier in 1828.

L. concinnus

L. havardii

L. perennis

L. plattensis

L. texensis

L. subcarnosus

Natural distribution of the six species of *Lupinus*.
Records or sightings outside these areas are probably
introductions. (Based on a 1985 map by B. L. Turner)

3 *Topview.*

2

1.
First to emerge from the seed,
in early October, are the primary root
and two seed leaves (cotyledons).
2.
Expanding root and shoot (stems and
leaves) systems follow within a week.
3.
A rosette of leaves hugs the ground
throughout the fall and winter.
4.
At the first warming of spring the
plant sends up bloom stalks.
5.
As each fertilized floret fades, a seed
pod forms in its place. About eight months
after stage 1 the pods explode (dehise),
catapulting the seed to the soil to begin
the life cycle once more.

4

1

GROWTH STAGES

5

[28]

Cultivating Bluebonnets

*I*n discussing the cultivation of bluebonnets, we will consider only *L. texensis* since seeds and plants of this species are available commercially. The bluebonnet is a cool-weather annual, which means it will require heat in order to germinate but cool weather to develop the root structure. The hard seeds look like tiny bits of gravel and are varicolored from light tan to slate blue. Their hard, tough lacquerlike coat helps the seeds to survive. In their natural habitat the seeds must be able to endure a broiling Texas summer.

Even though it may seem too hot for you to think about spring, start getting ready to plant bluebonnet seeds in September. The end of September through the second week in November is the best time to plant them, but planting can begin the first week in September and continue through early December. To avoid disappointment next spring it is necessary to plant inoculated seed. This is important because bluebonnets require the presence of certain bacteria for their root system to form the nodules that carry on the nitrogen-fixation process. An inoculant containing the bacteria can be purchased at commercial seed stores; however, it must be specific for *Lupinus texensis* and not just a general legume inoculant.

The Texas Department of Highways and Public Transportation recommends a seeding rate of 10–12 pounds per acre for long-range viewing. At this rate, an ounce (which would contain somewhere between 875 and 1,000 seeds) will cover a little over 200 square feet. This is about 5 seeds per square foot. With this seeding rate, maximum display would probably be reached the second or third year after planting. For small display areas in your garden or landscape to be viewed at close range, or in places where you want a good display more quickly, seed companies recommend that you use a little more seed, about 8 seeds per square foot. At this rate, an ounce would cover about 135 square feet. An acre would require 20 pounds.

The late Carroll Abbott, one of the first native plant specialists in Texas, believed that bluebonnet seeds, out in nature, needed three to five years for the hard coat to soften sufficiently for germination to take place. Most people don't want to wait that long, so what you have to do is to help nature along. He recommended scarification, a technique of scratching or rupturing the tough coating of the seed to accelerate germination.

A second means of accelerating germination is by soaking the seeds overnight in warm water. This may be done for several days if the water is changed daily. A combination of the two methods can be used: scratch then soak.

Now that you know how to scarify seed, forget it in the case of bluebonnets except for small flowerbeds. As a means of helping nature along, the Texas Highway Department and the National Wildflower Research Center do not, I repeat, do not recommend the process for any of the state flowers of Texas. Getting the seed to germinate is not the problem. Nodulation is the question. You could get one thousand seeds to germinate but, if only twenty are inoculated with *Rhizobium,* only twenty are going to blossom.

This failure to form nodules is the basis for another bluebonnet misconception. Many hold the belief that bluebonnets do not bloom the first year because they have planted the seeds, watched them germinate and grow into lush plants, but . . . no blooms. Nor will they bloom the second year. In fact, they will never bloom unless the seeds become inoculated with *Rhizobium.*

Once the essential bacterium is established, it will spread in the soil, but its presence is critical. Most current researchers working on this problem agree on one thing . . . INOCULATION. To do otherwise with your bluebonnet seed is to put out a lot of expensive bird feed.

Bluebonnet authorities are not just trying to be perverse when they preach "Do Not Scarify"; they have a good reason. If you made a large planting of scarified seed that produced 90–100 percent germination in a situation dependent on the natural elements, your bluebonnet crop would be subject to 100 percent kill if those elements were unfavorable. A freeze or failure to rain at required intervals could cause a costly disaster. However, if you allowed the seeds to germinate at their natural rate, such stepped intervals would reduce the risk of total seed loss.

Now, this caution need not apply to a small area in your home garden where you have control over the water supply and can protect the seedlings from cold and pests during the period needed for them to become established. Go ahead and scarify these seeds if you are going to be around to nurse the seedlings; just don't take a vacation until they get growing. I find that by putting the seeds in an electric blender jar and giving them three or four quick whirls, then soaking them overnight in warm water, I will have a high percentage of germination. Don't forget to inoculate your seeds while they are still damp! Seed scarified too far in advance of the actual planting date will dry out and fail to germinate. Buying prescarified seed is an iffy proposition, which also increases the vulnerability to insect damage.

To ensure success, you should also treat the seed with a fungicide to minimize damping-off of the seedlings. The application of both fungicide and inoculant to the seed can be performed in one operation (pelleting) just before planting. During its 1981 Wildflower Works Project, the Dallas Museum of Natural History staff demonstrated that pelleted bluebonnet seed produced plants more luxuriant in size and health than unpelleted seed.

Like most Texans, bluebonnets like the sun; they will not do well in the shade. They prefer soil that is well drained, sweet (alkaline, containing lime), and of moderate fertility. Scatter the seeds over a prepared seedbed and cover lightly with soil no more than one-half inch deep. Walk over or tamp your seedbed in order for the seeds to make good contact with the soil. Seed-soil contact is imperative. A firm seedbed is required for germination. If you are planting the seeds in a large area where it is not possible or practical to prepare a seedbed or to cover the seeds with soil, try to loosen the soil before broadcasting the seeds, then mow the existing vegetation so that it will fall and provide a covering for the seeds. Bluebonnet seeds must also have darkness to germinate.

Water your bluebonnet patch thoroughly but gently in order not to dislodge the seeds. Unless you get a good rain a few days

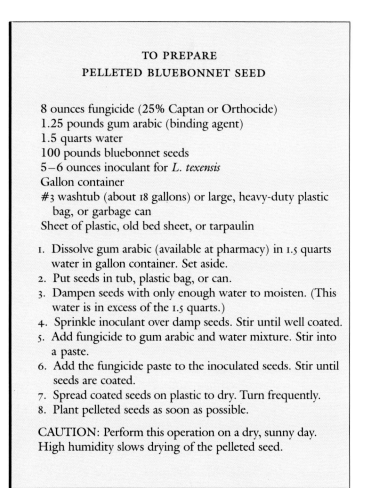

TO PREPARE
PELLETED BLUEBONNET SEED

8 ounces fungicide (25% Captan or Orthocide)
1.25 pounds gum arabic (binding agent)
1.5 quarts water
100 pounds bluebonnet seeds
5–6 ounces inoculant for *L. texensis*
Gallon container
#3 washtub (about 18 gallons) or large, heavy-duty plastic
   bag, or garbage can
Sheet of plastic, old bed sheet, or tarpaulin

1. Dissolve gum arabic (available at pharmacy) in 1.5 quarts
   water in gallon container. Set aside.
2. Put seeds in tub, plastic bag, or can.
3. Dampen seeds with only enough water to moisten. (This
   water is in excess of the 1.5 quarts.)
4. Sprinkle inoculant over damp seeds. Stir until well coated.
5. Add fungicide to gum arabic and water mixture. Stir into
   a paste.
6. Add the fungicide paste to the inoculated seeds. Stir until
   seeds are coated.
7. Spread coated seeds on plastic to dry. Turn frequently.
8. Plant pelleted seeds as soon as possible.

CAUTION: Perform this operation on a dry, sunny day.
High humidity slows drying of the pelleted seed.

after planting, the watering should be repeated within a week. The seeds will begin germinating by the end of the week and will continue for many weeks to come. DO NOT FERTILIZE your bluebonnets.

In nature, toward the end of the first week of October, if you look closely in the meadows and along the roadways you will begin to see the first two tender, round, pale green leaves of this flowering plant (angiosperm). It is a dicot (dicotyledon) and like all dicots (*di,* two) has two embryonic leaves. Typically they have flower parts in fives and are herbaceous. These tender seedlings provide tempting feasts for pill "bugs," land-dwelling crustaceans. To keep them from wiping out your tasty seedlings, sprinkle the seedbed liberally with pill bug bait or a recommended pesticide.

Within the next week several additional leaves appear; then the young plant uses this early growth period to form a ground-hugging rosette. The entire plant will not be over an inch or so high, but the leaves will cover an area about the size of a salad plate. It is in this flattened rosette stage that the bluebonnets will pass the winter, during which time a strong, deep, nodule-festooned root system develops. These root nodules contain bacteria, which take nitrogen out of the air and change it to a form that the bluebonnet roots can assimilate. Associated plants and those that grow after the bluebonnets complete their life cycle also benefit from this natural nitrogen fertilizer.

Bluebonnet seedlings can be transplanted all during the fall and early winter. Abbott suggested Valentine's Day as the cut-off date for transplanting. For successful transplanting, it is important that the plant be moved when it is small, handled carefully, and replanted promptly. A gentle but thorough watering followed by a light mulching will help ensure success.

These rosettes have been observed "snuggling" and "slumbering." As we have already seen, bluebonnets have palmately compound leaves. Each leaf in the two most common species usually has five leaflets. When it gets cold the bluebonnet plant goes into action to prevent damage from freezing weather. Each of the two lower leaflets folds itself across the petiole, or "snuggles" up to the other. The two above do the same thing. The single top leaflet folds itself in the middle like a book. Even with these precautions it is possible for a bluebonnet to freeze but it can tolerate temperatures to $-29°$C ($-20°$F). Continued cold, however, can slow the growth progress enough to delay the blossoming period.

At the first signs of warm weather and lengthening days the center branches begin to grow and the long-awaited bloom stalks appear. The blossoming date is influenced to some degree by the weather. The earliest flowers usually open about the middle of March in the southern part of the state, but the first blooms may not show before May in the more northern sections. The showy blue flowers of bluebonnets are borne on terminal racemes. Each inflorescence bears from seven to over fifty flowers. An individual flower is fertile only for five to six days at most. The length of the blooming period is about one month. Many flowers must be produced per plant to maintain this extended blooming period.

In a home garden, pinching out the first flower bud as soon as it develops will force the plant to produce additional flower spikes, which increases the number of blooms and may extend flowering up to a month.

Seeds mature about six weeks after the last flowers fade. In Central Texas that means toward the end of May. These should be harvested from plants that you have selected and marked at the peak of bloom, before the seed pod sheds its seed. Each legume, or pod, bears from one to seven seeds. The larger, heavier seeds have a higher germination rate and produce seedlings with a greater survivalship, according to Schaal and Leverich.

Gather unopened, brownish seed pods and put them in a tightly closed paper bag so that when the seed pods dehise (explode) the flying seed will be retained within the bag. They will settle to the bottom making removal of the now spiraled dry pods an easy task. In nature the ripe pods audibly split into two corkscrewlike sections catapulting the seed with a force that sends the pelletlike missiles up to four meters (13+ ft.) from the parent plant. This is the reason bluebonnets appear in colonies in the wild as well as in your neighbor's yard. If you are around when it happens you cannot fail to hear your bluebonnet patch going "snap, crackle, pop."

Seeds may be planted immediately after harvest or may be stored in paper bags in a cool dry place. Abbott wrote that bluebonnet seed may be kept up to fifty years and still be viable. A good yield is seventy-five pounds per acre.

If you wait too long to collect the seeds you will have missed them, because most of the pods split over a relatively short period; afterward seed collection will be slim.

Do's and Don't's
for Growing Bluebonnets

Do collect or purchase seed as soon as available.
Do store seed in a porous container in a cool dry place
   until time to plant.
Do inoculate seed with *Rhizobium.**
Do select well-drained alkaline soil in full sun.
Do plant from late September through October (earlier or
   later, depending on weather).
Do plant in loosened top soil ¼ to ½ inch deep.
Do press seed down to ensure seed-soil contact.
Do water weekly—rain or sprinkler, whichever is available
   through first freeze. Begin weekly watering again in early
   March.
Do allow seed to fully mature before collecting and/or
   mowing.
Do leave at least one-half the seed in the field for reseeding.

Don't scarify seed.
Don't be in a hurry; two to three years are required to
   establish the necessary nitrogen-fixing *Rhizobium*
   bacteria.

*Absolutely essential!

—David Northington, Director
National Wildflower Research Center

Lupinus texensis, now the most common bluebonnet in Texas because it is easier to cultivate than the other species, has been spread by the Highway Department along the state's roadways far beyond its natural range. At the first signs of spring the center branches start to grow; the bloom stalks begin to appear in early March and usually peak the first two weeks of April. About six weeks after the last flowers fade the seeds mature. In the wild the ripe pods will "explode" to hurtle the seed away from the mother plant, leaving only empty spiraled pods. Seed must be collected before this takes place. Note the important rufflike nitrogen-fixing nodules on the roots; without these nodules the plant will not bloom.

Uses

*T*he bluebonnet is gaining use; however, economic botanists hardly consider it one of their own. Although the primary value of *Lupinus texensis* and its five cousins is esthetic or ornamental, we cannot disregard its other uses. We might even think of it as a psychotropic plant since it certainly alters our mood—we feel uplifted by it.

Where else in the world other than the state Capitol of Texas would the occasion of a visit from an American president find thousands of school children lining the Capitol roadway singing "America" as they showered President Theodore Roosevelt's pathway with bluebonnets, the official Texas flower, on that memorable April 6, 1905.

FOOD SOURCE

To begin with, the living bluebonnets are not a food for grazing animals, such as cattle or horses. They won't touch them. According to David Northington, the unpublished results of tests conducted near Junction, Texas, in the fall and winter of 1985–1986 found that deer will eat bluebonnets. However, there are other herbaceous plants they would select to eat before they consumed bluebonnets. It would seem, then, that when in a bind deer will resort to eating bluebonnets. But, just let a flock of sheep or a herd of goats into the pasture full of bluebonnets and they will chew them to the ground before you can say Davy Crockett. If it were not for the fact that bluebonnets are so beautiful and that they furnish nitrogen to the soil, they would be the bane of the ranchers whose cattle turn up their discerning noses at a field of seemingly succulent bluebonnets. There is a reason. According to Thomas J. Mabry, plant chemist (Department of Botany, University of Texas at Austin), the presence of toxic quinolizidine alkaloid—also known as lupine alkaloid—in bluebonnets and related plants makes these plants unpalatable to cattle and other herbivores. However, they are not deadly poisonous. R. M. Polhill and P. H. Raven report that they are infrequently cut and baled for fodder, but in general they are not used as food for animals. In some European countries lupine breeding programs have been successful in reducing the alkaloid level in lupines, thus making them more palatable to livestock, according to B. L. Turner.

ORNAMENTAL AND ESTHETIC

There are three agencies or individuals to whom we are indebted for the current general usage of bluebonnets as a unit in landscape design in our residential areas and our public spaces. These are, first and foremost, the Texas Highway Department, now known as the State Department of Highways and Public Transportation. The others are Lady Bird Johnson (Mrs. Lyndon B.) and the late Carroll Abbott.

The State Department of Public Transportation and Highways, more commonly called the Highway Department, is responsible for the beautiful bluebonnets along the roadways of Texas. Within the Highway Department the highway commissioner, the state highway engineer, and the landscape architect are responsible for formulating the designs and directives that are put into operation by the departmental maintenance sections. This all began about 1932 when Judge W. R. Ely of Abilene was commissioner, Gibb Gilchrist was engineer, and Jack Gubbels was architect. Ely and Gilchrist hired Gubbels, the Highway Department's first landscape architect. Gubbels worked out the program, and the maintenance sections have been seeding, reseeding, and spreading bluebonnets ever since. William Pape, Sr., section foreman, is credited with scattering the first wild flower seed along US 77 near La Grange.

The world-renowned Texas naturalist Roy Bedichek declared what the Highway Department has done to be "the most conscious work in conservation of natural beauty on a grand scale that is being done at all, overshadowing in extent, as it certainly does in influence on the public mind, even park systems, state and national."

The beautification program, which is under the vegetation management program, has a fourfold purpose. The most obvious one, of course, is to add scenic beauty along the state's highways. The others are safety, utility, and economy. The value of the beautification-safety program and its direct relationship to reduced maintenance costs are now widely recognized. The money saved, $8 million in 1983, is a direct result of an innovative selective-mowing design, which will be operational in all 254 counties by 1988.

The success of the Texas wild flower planting program prompted federal legislation of a similar nature sponsored by Congressman J. J. Pickle and Senator Lloyd Bentsen of Texas. Known as the "National Wildflower Landscaping Act of 1985," the bill, H.R. 2878, will encourage the use of native wild flowers in highway landscaping throughout the United States.

The central office of the Texas State Department of Highways and Public Transportation is located in Austin, Texas 78701, at Eleventh and Brazos, right by the Capitol. They are real friendly people!

The undisputed queen of wild flowers in America is Texas' own first lady, Lady Bird Johnson, the wife of Lyndon Baines Johnson, the thirty-sixth president of the United States. Mrs. Johnson has done more to focus attention on bluebonnets and other wild flowers than anyone in America. We can add little to the citation from the Medal of Freedom she received in 1977: "Her leadership transformed the American landscape and preserved its natural beauty as a national treasure." Just when her interest in wild flowers began is hard to say, but it just didn't happen overnight . . . even the White House china commissioned during the Johnson administration bore bluebonnets and other wild flowers.

Public interest in beautification was aroused when Mrs. Johnson, as the president's wife, took official notice of accomplishments of the Texas Highway Department. In 1969, at a ceremony at the LBJ State Park, she made the first presentation of her personal check to the winner of a competition among maintenance workers in various departmental districts in Texas.

Born Claudia Alta Taylor in Karnack, Texas, on December 22, 1912, she became known at an early age as Lady Bird. There is not space to repeat here all of her accomplishments but only to recognize and thank her again for the seeds she has planted, and especially for making wild flowers and their propagation and conservation a part of the American consciousness.

In December 1982, on the occasion of her seventieth birthday, she took the lead in the establishment of a national wild flower research center on the Colorado River southeast of Austin, Texas, by contributing sixty acres of land and $125,000 to the cause of wild flower research. This young organization has impressive goals and is actively working toward their fulfillment. (New members are always welcome; contact the National Wildflower Research Center, 2600 FM 973 North, Austin, TX 78725.)

The enigmatic Carroll Abbott was a late bloomer. In 1970, at age 44, he abandoned his career as a political public relations consultant in Houston and packed his family off to Kerrville, Texas, the heart of the hills. From that day until his death in 1984 he and his family struggled to make ends meet while he tried to educate the public on how to propagate native flowers. He hoped to create a market for the wild flower seeds they were so diligently collecting for their Green Horizons, a mail order firm specializing in native plants.

Despite all of his problems, Abbott kept building his seed stockpiles and collecting notes for a book he later published, which has become the prime reference for many wild flower enthusiasts in Texas. He edited and published the award-winning quarterly *Texas Wild Flower Newsletter*. Abbott was also the moving force behind the establishment of an official State Wild Flower Day each April 24.

His untimely death brought an end to his colorful career, but he left an equally colorful legacy of bloom, which will be a perpetual memorial to a man who had loved wild flowers since he was a little boy.

Top: This undated Turneresque *Bluebonnets in Texas* (42⅝″ × 54⅝″) by Julian Onderdonk was a gift to the Lyndon Baines Johnson Library, Austin, Texas, in 1969 by Stanley Marcus of Dallas, Texas. *Bottom:* This 1948 landscape (28″ × 34″) by Porfirio Salinas, from the collection of Gen. and Mrs. John Coleman Horton of Austin, Texas, is one of many Salinas works acquired by Mrs. Horton's parents, Mr. and Mrs. Sully B. Roberdeau.

Art Historian Joe Frantz states that "bluebonnet painting is practically a pastoral rite in Texas, a sort of Lone Star *sacre du printemps.*" Unfortunately, bluebonnet painting has fallen into disrepute and has become the brunt of myriad jokes about Sunday painters, most well deserved. It is almost impossible to do justice to something already as beautiful as a sunset, a rainbow, or a bluebonnet, but two Texas artists have come close. If you have not seen the work of Julian Onderdonk and Porfirio Salinas, make the effort. They are the models all those others are trying to copy.

A native Texan and the son of a German immigrant, Julian Onderdonk was born in San Antonio on July 30, 1882. He not only studied with his artist father, Robert, but, like his sire, he also trained at the Art Students League in New York. Perhaps more influential than his teachers at the League was the tutelage of William Merritt Chase, whose style can be traced in Onderdonk's painting.

When young Onderdonk returned to Texas in 1909, he took over his father's position as curator of art exhibitions for the annual Dallas State Fair. He poured the rest of his energy into painting the vast expanses and sweeping vistas of his beloved Texas. He was primarily a landscape artist and is remembered best for his depictions of Texas bluebonnets. During his brief lifetime his work became very popular, engendering a multitude of imitators.

A Texan of Mexican ancestry, Porfirio Salinas was born just after the turn of the century in the little Central Texas town of Bastrop. When he was very young he moved to San Antonio. Unlike his predecessor and inspiration, Onderdonk, Salinas had no formal art training but learned his technique from his associates at the paint store where he was employed and by careful observation and practice. Having chosen bluebonnets as his special concentration, he could not have followed a better example than Onderdonk. The self-taught Salinas became a legend within his lifetime. Many think that he is the premier artist of the southwestern region. "Suffice it to say that no other painter in the history of that region has been so thoroughly recognized by the buying public," according to Frantz.

Landscape Design   Inspired and led by an enlightened and foresighted Highway Department program, the first in the nation, to plant wild flowers and native plants along state roadways, landscape designers throughout the state and the nation are using bluebonnets and other wild flowers in their plans. Not only is this trend providing vistas of awe-inspiring beauty for our populace but it also has proven to be highly significant in water conservation and highway maintenance, not only considerably curtailing the amount of water and labor involved but also reducing the cost to Texas tax payers. Once established, bluebonnets are a long-lasting, low-maintenance addition to any landscape plan, adding not only color but also fragrance.

These low-growing annuals are used mostly in large areas where their colorful impact can best be felt, but their importance as a border or bedding plant should not be disregarded. The ease of maintaining a stand of bluebonnets has caused them to be introduced into parks, street medians, airport grounds, cemeteries, church yards, public buildings, shopping centers, and rights-of-way, around mailboxes, and at approaches to ranches as well as in the home garden. A Dallas-based artist has even designed and produced massive "Wildflower Works" employing living wild flowers best viewed from the air like the Pre-Columbian Nasca lines in Peru. In 1981 the Dallas Museum of Natural Science and the Dallas/Fort Worth International Airport produced Wildflower Works, which demonstrated in living color that native plant material can be used in urban environments.

Decorative Motif   If visitors to Texas should happen into a souvenir shop or gift shop they would soon be overwhelmed with the bluebonnet. It has become a symbol of Texas and is used as a decorative motif on almost everything from cheap ashtrays to the finest china. It is currently running the risk of becoming trivialized by overcommercialization.

Oversized bluebonnets, tiny bluebonnets, spindly bluebonnets, distorted bluebonnets, even pretty bluebonnets are everywhere. Nothing is sacred. Stationery, note paper, postcards, napkins, and paper plates and cups are a few of the paper products enlivened by its image. Pottery, china, crystal, vases, linens, towels, placemats, napkins, and even a lace-bedecked boudoir pillow embroidered with bluebonnets and the words "A Texan loves you" are some of the household items embellished with bluebonnets. To say nothing of wallpaper, upholstery fabrics, wall hangings, tapestries, dress fabrics, calendars, and framed prints bearing its likeness. Some are tasteful, some hideous, but all inspired by the beautiful Texas lupines. At the Dallas Trade Mart a buyer will soon discover that the bluebonnet is big business.

Photographs on pages 48–49, except silk flowers, courtesy of Foley's, Houston, Texas.

SANDY WILSON PHOTO

BLUEBONNET
Lupinus texensis

Photography   Come spring, on a day when the sun is bright and the clouds their fluffiest, a peculiar exodus from Texas cities takes place. Everyone packs up and sallies forth to a favorite bluebonnet patch with loved ones and cameras. People are not the only creatures that sally forth at bluebonnet time. Snakes begin emerging from winter hibernation at the same signs of spring. One of the more aggressive of the venomous snakes is the western diamondback rattler. Warn your children and be on guard when walking through the dense foliage of a bluebonnet patch. If you do encounter a snake you think may be poisonous, slowly back away the way you came. If you should get bitten, seek medical attention as soon as possible.

If you don't believe that Texans love their bluebonnets, just look at the number of vehicles idling along any bluebonnet-bordered roadway in Texas during the first two weeks of April when the blue in Texans' blood is stirring and they take to the road to pay homage to their favorite flower. The film manufacturers must wonder what is taking place in the Lone Star State that boosts their sales so at that time.

For almost thirty years the little town of Marlin held a Bluebonnet Photo Fiesta; for some reason it was discontinued in the mid-sixties. It was probably too popular, because in 1985 the *Austin American-Statesman,* in answer to a request that readers send in their choice bluebonnet pictures, received 2,612 photographs from more than 800 readers.

The treasured photos arrived wrapped in tissue, ledger paper, colored stationery, boxes, manila envelopes, and plastic bags. They were of every size and shape imaginable. Some carried handwritten stories or typed script. The newspaper reported that

> there were ferrets in the bluebonnets, goats in the bluebonnets, Texas flags and teddy bears, brides, and rainbows in the bluebonnets. There were all sorts of pets—kittens, cats, afghan hounds, rabbits, sheepdogs, horses. There were kids with their animals, kids with their stuffed toys, and Cabbage Patch Kids all by themselves, even armadillos.

Many of the photographs were faded, out of focus, but the smiles and the flowers seemed just as glowing. They had all had a good day.

Bluebonnets are notoriously difficult to photograph. The blue absorbs so much light that faces and light clothing are usually overexposed. Most have a disappointing blue or they are blurred because the wind blows the blossoms. There are so many variables that it is hard to get it all together.

Here are a few suggestions from personal experience.

Concerning movement—wind doesn't blow constantly. Be patient and be all set to snap when it subsides. This works well with landscapes and adults—children and pets are another problem.

Subjects should wear clothing the same value (lightness or darkness) as the bluebonnets, avoiding white and light colors to prevent overexposure. Shooting at early morning or late afternoon will help to cut down on the squinting. Avoid midday; the overhead light will let the brows shade the eyes too much and will drain color.

For sharper results in landscapes, focus about midway in your field, using the smallest aperture possible.

If you don't like the background when making a close-up of the blossoms or faces, use your largest aperture. This will put the undesirable background material out of focus.

I try to avoid recommending particular products, but for me the color quality has been so improved when I use Fugii 400 color print film that I can't refrain from suggesting that you try it if you've had disappointing color prints. With slides there is little difference.

Use a tripod. You may not be as steady as you think you are.

Send the film to a reliable processor or to the manufacturer for processing. Request that the prints be printed on the warm side. Most places process all film the same way but there are processors who give special attention. If you get one of those once-in-a-lifetime shots of baby sister in a field of blue, spend a little extra to get your negative printed by a good lab.

Now, say cheese! Please.

Bluebonnets need not be broken off and jammed into the first handy fruit jar. I arranged and photographed this orientally influenced contemporary design to present a different approach with an economy of plant material that becomes an integral part of the container of my own design and construction.

Flower Arranging So many bluebonnets are cultivated in home gardens today that we may freely cut them for enjoyment inside the home as well as outside. Although it is not against the law, refrain from taking them from natural sources. If you plan to cut the blossoms for use in flower arranging, cut the stems as long as possible. Strip the leaves from the lower part of the stem before putting in water. If foliage is left below the water line its decomposition will foul the water, thereby shortening the cut life of the blooms. Next take a bucket or tall container and plunge the cut flowers in the water up to the blossoms. Allow them to remain thus for several hours. This is called "hardening" and is a technique for extending the cut life of the plant material. It also allows the stem to take the shape it will maintain before you make your arrangement instead of changing its shape after you have incorporated it into your design.

The bluebonnet lends itself to any floral design style from the typical massed arrangement in a white ironstone pitcher to any of the more exotic oriental types. Don't be afraid to experiment. Your family and guests will enjoy your efforts and they should stay pretty for about a week if you follow the precautions given here.

If you should want to have bluebonnets in your bridal bouquet or in those of your bridesmaids you will have to pick them yourself and take them to a florist. It is the state flower and cannot be sold by dealers. First, harden it as directed. Should you be a strict environmentalist, substitute silk bluebonnets in floral arrangements.

ENTERTAINMENT AND TOURISM

Entertainment??? No, bluebonnets don't sing and dance but they certainly do inspire the people who love them to do all sorts of things, some of them pretty weird. We have a Bluebonnet Bowl in Houston where top-ranking Texas gladiators

meet their opponents every New Year's Eve, bluebonnet festivals, bluebonnet queens, bluebonnet beauty pageants, bluebonnet fun runs, bluebonnet art and crafts shows, bluebonnet
trails, historic home tours. People make love in bluebonnets,
and people get married in bluebonnets. I'm sure glad they
don't grow six feet tall; no telling what would happen in a bluebonnet patch if you could hide. During springtime in Texas the
bluebonnet show is truly the Biggest Show on Earth.

Trails Bluebonnets are concentrated in three principal areas
in Texas. The residents of these areas capitalize on the beauty of
their region at blooming time with highly organized festivals
and special activities along marked trails so that the visitors can
really make a day or a weekend out of their visit. These usually
occur during the first two weeks of April. Sometimes the bluebonnets are a little earlier, sometimes a little later, but unless
there has been a drought lasting several years there will always
be some. The marked trails are:

The Coastal Trail
The Houston Bluebonnet Trail (with Brenham at its center)
The Highland Lakes Bluebonnet Trail

The Coastal Trail runs along the Gulf coast of Texas from Indianola and Port Lavaca through Palacios to Bay City and
Edna. It is usually the earliest of the three.

The Houston Bluebonnet Trail forms a circle with Brenham
at its center and U.S. 290 bisecting it. Houston is the nearest
big city. This is a very historic area of Texas and includes the
site of the first capital of the state, Washington on the Brazos,
with its state park. The circle's perimeter passes through Sealy,
Columbus, La Grange, Giddings, Caldwell, Bryan, Navasota,
and Hempstead.

The Highland Lakes Bluebonnet Trail works its way out of
the present-day capital of the state at Austin, traveling north-
west, past the lakes formed by the damming of the Colorado
River. You will pass through Burnet, Kingsland, Buchanan

Dam, Llano, and Marble Falls. This is a very highly organized affair, with something going on in each of these small towns.

Besides these trails, Ennis, just south of Dallas on Interstate 45, has a Bluebonnet Trail and Walkfest, and Kenedy, on U.S. 181 southeast of San Antonio, puts on a Bluebonnet Day Festival.

I'd like to add another route that is a favorite of mine, but not organized. Drive on U.S. 183 south from Austin to Lockhart and Luling. Here there is a wider mixture of spring blossoms with the bluebonnets. Plan to eat some Texas barbeque in Lockhart; it's famous!

Don't forget to take U.S. 290 West to Johnson City and Fredericksburg. The Lyndon B. Johnson Park across the road from his ranch home on the Pedernales River gets prettier every year.

Watch the newspapers in these regions. They can be depended on for maps, dates, lists of events, times, and so on. If you should miss that information source, call any one of the chambers of commerce in the towns listed. These people will be happy to send you maps and programs of events. Or write to:

Highland Lakes
Tourist Association
P.O. Box 1967
Austin, TX 78767
Tel. 512/478-9383

Washington County
Chamber of Commerce
314 South Austin
Brenham, TX 77833

Don't feel too bad if you can't make one of these trails because in springtime there are bluebonnets all over the state, perhaps not as abundant or with the attendant festivities but equally beautiful. The Highway Department makes a continuing effort to spread them along every right-of-way in the state and that's a lot. It includes one million acres. That's *beaucoup* bluebonnets!

Speaking of trails, how about one from San Antonio to St. Louis? According to J. K. Maguire, that was the route of the crack Katy Railroad train known as *The Bluebonnet*, the only train ever operated in the United States named for a wild flower.

Festivals and Pageants   Each year there are more bluebonnet-time festivities. We will cite only two but those interested can watch the newspapers at the end of March and in early April or the official state travel magazine *Texas Highways,* which has a monthly "Fun Forecast" cataloging all the goings-on by region. Self-addressed envelopes to the Bluebonnet Editor, *Southern Living,* Box 523, Birmingham, AL 35201, may produce additional information.

Beginning in 1965, a Texas Bluebonnet Queen has been crowned by the governor of Texas each spring in Austin. This social event at the governor's mansion is sponsored by the Texas Bluebonnet Committee, Inc., a nonprofit organization whose goals include planting and spreading bluebonnet seed and encouraging bluebonnet trails. The members sell a fabric called "Texas Bluebonnet Tartan" to aid their projects.

In the hills at Burnet, the Bluebonnet Pageant has been held each spring since 1961. Reigning over this event are Miss Burnet Bluebonnet, Junior Miss Bluebonnet, Ideal Miss Bluebonnet, and Little Miss Bluebonnet.

POETRY AND SONG

Poetry has always been one of humankind's means of expressing its innermost feelings about things and events and emotions. Many odes to the bluebonnet have been written. Those by Sjolander, Mims, Houston, and Booth have been admired. But, like paintings of bluebonnets, all I have seen have fallen short of what I think a paean to bluebonnet time should be. Would that Wordsworth had seen the bluebonnet before he viewed the daffodil!

In an excess of zeal but in honor of the bluebonnet, the Forty-third Legislature in 1933 adopted a state flower song called "Bluebonnets," with words by Julia D. Booth and music by Lora C. Crockett (see pages 62–63).

LITERATURE

Myths and Legends Perhaps the bluebonnet has not yet become a full-fledged cult object but it has been the subject of several myths and legends. At one time those who held that something so beautiful could not be native to a place like Texas would have us believe that it had been brought to our hills by the Spanish who had acquired the seeds from priests who had obtained them while making a pilgrimage to the Holy Land or it had been brought to Texas in shipments of grain or clover from the Mediterranean countries. Botanists, such as Turner, have given those doubters their comeuppance by proving that bluebonnets are native to Texas and occurred here before the first Spaniard ever set his boot on a Texas prairie. Johnston explains that the European bluebonnet is quite another flower, while the bluebonnet of Southern California is *Lupinus affinus* Agardh, according to R. Caldwell.

There are those writers who would have us believe that these stories originated with the early Spanish missionaries to Texas in their efforts to placate the Indians and keep them hanging around the missions. However, I think legends are like Aggie jokes; no one ever knows just who started them.

I will summarize, somewhat irreverently, a few of them that have been published. All but one of these involve Indians and we all know that in the days before central heat and T.V., Amerindians spent a lot of time sitting around campfires spinning yarns and invoking the Great Spirit.

The first legend is from an Austin newspaper (April 1964). If you have ever wondered, as you gazed out over a field of azure bluebonnets and scarlet Indian paintbrush, how they came to be, then wonder no more, "cuz," *Once upon a time* . . . there lived an aged chief and his tribe in a land of ice and mountainous rock. It was a time of starvation and suffering. The chief ascended to a high place and entreated his ancestor beyond the cold sun (shades of those lands west of the Bering Strait).

Then came "a voice from afar." It is sufficient to say that he took the message to his people, with the result that they followed him on and on, through thick and thin, until they found the place the Great Spirit had told them to seek. This being a bluebonnet book, the land would be recognized because "in each season of the bud, it will be covered with blossoms—as many as falling rain—and all, of the sky's pure color."

All of this didn't happen overnight. The original old chief who received the message went to his happy hunting ground. This scenario was repeated through many generations of chiefs before they finally reached the promised land of blue flowers where they set up their village and hunted and gathered. At the time of the blue flowers the old chief came down and told the young chief that the blue flowers would come each year as a sign that "our people have remained true and just and honorable." This prophecy was passed on from father to son and the people remained good.

However, these good people finally became lazy and ornery. The bluebonnets became pale and enemies came and all that. The current chief found himself one of those high places and went up for a little palaver with the spirit of his father, who evidently told him to fetch a big brush and a lot of red earth so he could paint as many of those blue blossoms red as he could. Which he did.

Next morning an enemy appeared among the blue flowers. The young chief's people were soft from the good life and took to the woods, but a bunch of strangers with red faces (as many as the flowers the father had painted) took up spears and drove the enemy away, then vamoosed. The young chief went to the field of blossoms splashed with red and found his father's brush.

The people returned. Now that they had the big brush and the red earth and the secret they figured they had it made. Paying no attention to their blue blossoms, they went about having a big time. What ho? Another enemy cometh!

They ran for the paint brushes and starting spreading the red paint around. No luck. When the enemy departed this time the remaining people wept and died in the blossoms they had made red. The chief fell, clutching a blue flower. Across the face of the flower was a faint white mark, "like an Indian's tear from long-ago snows."

"Today, when the moon is right, in the season of the bud, the old ones say you can hear the last despairing chief across the plains and by the water and over the meadows as he bends among the blue flowers he paints red."

The second legend, which appeared in a Houston newspaper (July 21, 1935), is about an Aztec Indian maiden. The Aztecs lived somewhat south of the bluebonnet belt, but in legends anything goes.

Once upon a time . . . a beautiful little Aztec maiden offered her life in atonement for her people's sins. As she was being led to the sacrificial altar, her blue headdress fell to the earth and the Great Spirit, in compassion, caused thousands of blue flowers to spring up in commemoration of the brave and tragic young Indian virgin.

Another of the bluebonnet legends, claimed for the Creeks by Hyaka Hvtcuce, has been made into a colorful children's book as well as having been set down by Dobie in his *Tales of Old-Time Texas*. It is as sentimental as the others, nevertheless.

Once upon a time . . . a great drought had fallen on the land and everything was dying. Again, the local chief sought out a high place and consulted with the Great Spirit after the people had exhausted themselves with dancing and incantation for rain.

The Great Spirit pronounced that the people should offer up to the flames their most valued possession, and the ashes of this offering must be scattered to the four winds. Until this sacrifice was made, their drought and famine would continue.

In this tribe was a little orphan girl called "She-Who-Is-Alone." Little Orphan S-W-I-A had as her only possession a beloved warrior doll all dressed up with a headdress of blue jay feathers. Poor little S-W-I-A listened to her elders and watched all their maneuvers trying to break the drought and heard what the Great Spirit had told these selfish people to do if they wanted things to get better. She thought and she thought. She mulled and she mulled, as little girls with warrior dolls do. At last, she knew what to do.

After all the folks had gone to bed she ran up to THE HIGH PLACE and called to the Great Spirit. There, all alone, by the light of the prairie moon, she offered up her doll, saying, "O Great Spirit, here is my warrior doll. It is the only thing I have from my family who died in this famine. It is my most valued possession. Please accept it." Then she tippy-toed back to the embers of the camp fire. Taking a few of the glowing coals she went out into the hills and built a fire and offered her little doll with the blue feathers to the flames. After the flames died out, she scattered the ashes as she had been instructed, and then she fell asleep from the whole effort.

Guess what?

When she awoke and stretched and looked around . . . lo and behold, on the ground where the ashes had fallen was a blanket of beautiful blue flowers. The people finally awakened and saw this sight. Rain began to fall. They danced and gave thanks. From that day on, the little girl was known by another name—"One-Who-Dearly-Loves-Her-People."

"And every spring, the Great Spirit remembers the sacrifice of a little girl and fills the hills and valleys of the land, now called Texas, with the beautiful blue flowers. Even to this day."

A change of pace with a non-Indian tale, which, for some unexplained reason, takes place in Louisiana, according to Mary Daggett Lake.

Once upon a time . . . in the river city of New Orleans, a grieving lover stabbed himself to death on the grave of his sweetheart in the St. Roch cemetery. His blood spattered onto the clover. Today, if you look closely at the older flowers on a bluebonnet stalk, you will see blood-red splotches on each banner petal above the two keel-like petals. It is the way the bluebonnet immortalized the devotion of the fallen lover.

Once upon a time . . . two neighboring Indian tribes were waging a big battle, R. A. Selle tells us. They fought unto death. Even after all of the braves entered the happy hunting ground they continued the fierce fighting. It was so violent that they knocked great hunks from the blue sky. When the slabs of sky hit the earth, they shattered into tiny pieces, which turned into bluebonnets.

Another from Selle: *Once upon a time* . . . Blue Blanket, a great chief, led his braves in a raid on another tribe. Amongst the plunder and loot brought back to their camp was a beautiful maiden named Blue Song. When their chief saw her, he had to have her for his new wife. He ordered the old wives to wait on Blue Song so that she could sit around and sing to him all day.

Blue Song made herself a lovely blue headdress and spent her days singing to Chief Blue Blanket while being waited on by the senior wives. The couple lived to a great age and pleased the Great Spirit exceedingly. As a sign of his pleasure, the Great Spirit spread the emblem of his favorite tribe—a beautiful blue blanket—over the hills and the prairies.

And the last, again by Selle: *Once upon a time* . . . a terrible fire swept the prairie, destroying and blackening everything in its path. The people fled to the Mission to save themselves from the sweeping blaze. Soon there was no food.

Hearing of their plight, the Great Spirit sent them a beautiful blue bird to be sacrificed to the gods. He admonished them not to burn the feathers of the bird but to plant each of the blue plumes on the blackened hillsides. And they did. And it worked! Rain came. The ashes were washed away as each feather grew into a lovely blue plume-like blossom.

End of legends. Take your choice. In any case, the bluebonnets will always return each spring to bless the people.

THANK YOU, GREAT SPIRIT,
FOR THE BLUEBONNET.

BLUEBONNETS

JULIA D. BOOTH

LORA COSTON CROCKETT

When the pas - tures are green in the spring - time And the
Blue - bon - nets so gor - geous and state - ly In your

birds — are sing ing their son - nets, You may
man - tel of blue and of green, — In the

look to the hills and the val - leys And they're
spring when you're in your full glo - ry You're the

cov - ered with love - ly blue bon - nets.
lov - li - est sight ev - er seen. —

Blue is the em-blem of loy - al - ty, They're as blue as the deep deep
You're beauti-ful when you sway in the sunshine, You look like the waves of the

sea, Their smil - ing fac - es bring
sea, Ah Tex - as was wise in her

glad - ness For they bloom for you and for me.
choice of a flow'r So we of-fer our hom - age to thee.

CHORUS

Blue-bon-nets blue love-ly Blue-bon-nets, More beau-ti - ful

than all the rest. Tex - as chose you for her flow-er,

And so we love you best Blue-bon - nets.

Copyright 1932 by Lora Coston Crockett
International Copyright

Lampasas

US 183

US 281

FM
2241

Tow
Lake
Buchanan

Burnet

Bertram

I-35

Llano
Inks
Lake
P 4
FM 2342

TX 29

Georgetown

Kingsland

Marble Falls

Round Rock

FM
2900

Lake
Travis

FM 1431

TX 71

TX 6

Pedernales Falls
State Park

2222

Austin

Fredericksburg

Johnson
City

US 290

US 290

I-35

Luckenbach

Stonewall

Dripping
Springs

TX 60

US 59

TX 71

Edna

TX 111

TX 35

Bay City

US 59

TX 172

TX 60

TX 87

TX 35

TX 35

Palacios

Matagorda

Port Lavaca

Indianola

TX 35